Not by Bread Alone

Daily Reflections for Lent 2024

Catherine Upchurch

LITURGICAL PRESS
Collegeville, Minnesota

www.litpress.org

Nihil Obstat: Rev. Robert Harren, J.C.L., *Censor Librorum*

Imprimatur: ✠ Most Rev. Patrick M. Neary, C.S.C., Bishop of St. Cloud, May 9, 2023

Cover design by Monica Bokinskie. Cover art courtesy of Getty Images.

Scripture excerpts in this work are from the *Lectionary for Mass for Use in the Dioceses of the United States of America, second typical edition* © 2001, 1998, 1997, 1986, 1970 Confraternity of Christian Doctrine, Inc., Washington, DC. Used with permission. All rights reserved. No portion of this text may be reproduced by any means without permission in writing from the copyright owner.

Other Scripture texts in this work are taken from the *New American Bible, revised edition* © 2010, 1991, 1986, 1970 Confraternity of Christian Doctrine, Washington, DC and are used by permission of the copyright owner. All Rights Reserved. No part of the New American Bible may be reproduced in any form without permission in writing from the copyright owner.

© 2023 by Catherine Upchurch

Published by Liturgical Press, Collegeville, Minnesota. All rights reserved. No part of this book may be used or reproduced in any manner whatsoever, except brief quotations in reviews, without written permission of Liturgical Press, Saint John's Abbey, PO Box 7500, Collegeville, MN 56321-7500. Printed in the United States of America.

ISSN: 1552-8782 (print); 2692-6407 (e-book)

ISBN: 978-0-8146-6706-4   978-0-8146-6707-1 (e-book)

Introduction

The season of Lent is a season of the heart. It is a yearly reminder to check our pulse, to review what damages and what heals our hearts, as well as what quickens our hearts to reclaim our identity as sons and daughters of God.

You'll notice I did not say we check our *spiritual* pulse. The way we move about in the world is much more integrated than thinking of our spiritual well-being in isolation from other aspects of our identity. In many languages, especially in the ancient world where our biblical texts emerged, the "heart" is a shortcut way of talking about the core of what it means to be human. The heart is the home of emotions, yes, but it is also the home of intelligence, imagination, moral decision-making, and spiritual connection.

So, when I say this is a season of the heart, I mean this is a season that allows us to peer into the heart of our own humanity. What does it mean to ache and yearn for what we desire? How have we experienced emptiness, and how have we tried to fill it? What draws us to sin and sorrow when forgiveness and joy are so readily available? How do we measure our faithfulness, if it can be measured at all? Where have we experienced the presence of Christ? How has our own suffering weighed on us? And what have we done about the suffering of others?

Ultimately, this is a season when we consciously invite Christ to peer into our hearts with us, confident that he knows the human experience from the inside. He knows the importance of relationships, the desire to be understood, the yearning for freedom, and the challenge of responsibility. He knows that by stirring our imaginations and challenging our preconceptions, we can become free to love as he loves. He knows that by being with us in our sorrow, we can be healed, and by walking with us through storms, we can be strengthened.

Just as our physical health is a year-round responsibility, this once-a-year checkup keeps us on track. In this season of "heart health," we turn to God who inhabits our lives and has the power to transform them.

Catherine Upchurch

Reflections

February 14: Ash Wednesday

The Work of Lent

Readings: Joel 2:12-18; 2 Cor 5:20–6:2; Matt 6:1-6, 16-18

Scripture:
[R]eturn to me with your whole heart . . . (Joel 2:12)

Reflection: In the reports surrounding an act of violence that occurred in a public shopping center, one man commented to the press, "I could comprehend what was happening in my head, but I still can't grasp it in my heart." He talked about the measures he took to get himself and some other shoppers to a safe place. He recalled tamping down the sense of panic that was rising in his throat so he could do what was necessary. But his heart was having a hard time catching up.

Perhaps it is often this way—we feel our hearts are in a slightly different place than our minds. But that doesn't really seem to be the way we are made. Our hearts yearn to be part of the whole of our lives. In many ancient languages, references to the heart are references to the very core of what it means to be human. The heart is the seat of intellect, morality, physical health, imagination, and emotion. And so it is in Scripture.

We begin Lent by acknowledging that we have work to do, and that God is at work in us. Internally we submit ourselves to God to become wholehearted in devotion, and externally we express our identity through works that keep us aware of our connections to each other.

Our Gospel today assumes we do righteous deeds: "*When* you give alms, . . . *When* you pray, . . . *When* you fast, . . ." These are expression of a heart that is on a path to wholeness.

Meditation: In this season when we are called to focus on what separates us from God and from others, and on what heals these separations, we cry out to God in the words of the psalmist, "A clean heart create for me, O God, / . . . a willing spirit sustain in me." We invite God to put us back together whenever "parts" of ourselves seem to have trouble catching up.

Prayer: O God, look into our hearts and see what is out of rhythm with your desires for us. Do the mending our hearts need so our words and deeds can flow from your fullness.

February 15: Thursday after Ash Wednesday

Finding a Still Point

Readings: Deut 30:15-20; Luke 9:22-25

Scripture:
"Choose life, then, that you and your descendants may live, by loving the Lord, your God, heeding his voice, and holding fast to him." (Deut 30:19-20)

Reflection: In the world of science there is a natural phenomenon known as a "holdfast." It is most noticeable in ocean plants that swirl with the tides but stay firmly attached to the ocean floor. Scientists describe the knobby system of glue-like fingers that stick to rock and sand as a holdfast, produced by the plant's interaction with sunlight and salt water. That interaction creates an invisible bond that allows a plant like bullwhip kelp to stay in place even amid turbulent conditions.

The writer of Deuteronomy encourages God's people to find in the choice for life and love the holdfast that will anchor us throughout our lives. And while the choice is simple and clear, it is not an easy one. It requires bending our will to God's will in obedience. It requires that we be docile in our listening for God's voice and courageous in proclaiming the truth of who God is.

Choosing life and love will put us on the path of following Jesus, who is willing to suffer greatly and be rejected as we hear in today's Gospel. In the ultimate twist, by choosing love and choosing life, Jesus has to be willing to give up his own.

For Jesus and his followers, the cross becomes the holdfast in the eye of the storm. In the cross we discover that love looks like mercy and forgiveness, and that life springs from death.

Meditation: Throughout our Sacred Scriptures, there is a consistent call to listen for God's voice and to respond in loving obedience. In our hurried pace, and with so many competing messages in our culture, that kind of listening is hard to come by. Where will we find our still point if we fail to slow our steps, if we don't stop in our tracks to gaze at the cross, if we don't find in the cross the reason to choose life and love?

Prayer: Create in us, O God, the desire to hear your voice and the habits of stillness that can draw us deeply into your gifts of love and life.

February 16: Friday after Ash Wednesday

The Fasting God Desires

Readings: Isa 58:1-9a; Matt 9:14-15

Scripture:
For you are not pleased with sacrifices;
   should I offer a burnt offering, you would not accept it.
My sacrifice, O God, is a contrite spirit;
   a heart contrite and humbled, O God, you will not spurn.
      (Ps 51:18-19)

Reflection: When I was a child, a local religious leader encouraged the school children in our diocesan Catholic schools to give up cookies for Lent. The sacrifice, though small, would remind us that this was a season to honor the supreme sacrifice of Jesus. I never quite understood what a snickerdoodle, my personal favorite cookie, had to do with Jesus dying on a cross. Yet, all cookies disappeared for six long weeks from the school cafeteria.

Later in life, I was able to appreciate that this leader was trying to create a habit of sacrifice that was appropriate to our age level, a habit many of us continue in traditional fasts from things like chocolate, coffee, or alcohol during Lent. If these practices draw us closer to the God who desires a contrite and humble spirit from us, then they have meaning; if they do not, these practices can be empty at best, and dangerous at worst. They become dangerous when we trick ourselves into believing in a God who is concerned with what looks good rather than what creates good.

Today's readings challenge us to fast from attitudes and behaviors that divide us from one another. By focusing on our bonds with the hungry, the oppressed, the naked and homeless, we find healing for the woundedness of our world. We discover in the path of humility that our God is indeed with us.

Meditation: God's word is peppered with reminders that in our intimate connections with one another, in sharing in each other's struggles, we draw closer to the God who made us all. How might we sharpen our awareness of the conditions that cause oppression or diminish the dignity of human beings? How might this awareness create the humble and contrite spirit the psalmist speaks of?

Prayer: Lord God, I desire to know your ways. In my Lenten practices help me to deepen my commitment to loving you and loving my neighbor as myself.

February 17: Saturday after Ash Wednesday

Repairing the Breach

Readings: Isa 58:9b-14; Luke 5:27-32

Scripture:
. . . "Repairer of the breach," they shall call you . . . (Isa 58:12)

Reflection: When my father died, those of us who knew him best were well aware that as wonderfully generous as he could be in the community, he also carried within him some deep hurts—hurts he had caused and hurts he had suffered. At his funeral I spoke about our role as "repairers of the breach," the privilege and responsibility we have been given to share in another person's journey with honesty and compassion. In this way we acknowledge our shared humanity; in this way we help restore what is damaged.

The prophet Isaiah proclaims a word of encouragement to God's people in exile. Their inattention to God's covenant has paved the way to Babylon where they are estranged from all they once held dear. The prophet is aware of the deep chasm between who they professed to be and who they have become. The time of their exile is coming to an end, and Isaiah wants them to know that their future can be different. By attending to the oppressed and hungry, by speaking truth and heeding God's concerns, they can become repairers of the breach. God's people can live into who they are called to be, restoring the integrity of the human condition in the process.

The ministry of Jesus embodies this kind of restoration. He eats with tax collectors and other known sinners, aware of their need for restoration, generous in his ability to walk with them as the breach of sin is repaired and their brokenness is made whole.

Meditation: When we stop to examine our lives from the viewpoint of integrity, we may become aware of a certain amount of inconsistency between what we profess to value and what our daily priorities reveal. We might express this as our hearts feeling ill at ease. But our God draws together these disparate parts of ourselves when we acknowledge the need to be made whole.

Prayer: When we recognize the deep divide between who we are and who we desire to be, give us the courage, O God, to come to you to fill in the breach. Then send us out to be ministers of repair in our world.

February 18: First Sunday of Lent

The Time of Fulfillment

Readings: Gen 9:8-15; 1 Pet 3:18-22; Mark 1:12-15

Scripture:
"This is the time of fulfillment. The kingdom if God is at hand. Repent, and believe in the gospel." (Mark 1:15)

Reflection: Picture a little girl asking her parents, "When is the future?" As they struggle to respond with something sensible, they realize that when we reach the future, it is already the present. We never actually seem to catch the future.

Is this something that our ancestors in faith also struggled to grasp? They hoped for the restoration of the monarchy in Israel, a hope that transformed into waiting for the Messiah to come. But when would any of this ever be realized? Would it always remain a deep but vague hope for something out there, somewhere beyond time?

Our Gospel today finds Jesus telling those who would listen that the future is now: "This is the time of fulfillment." Did it feel that way? Jesus has just come from a long time of testing in the desert. John the Baptist has been imprisoned and will soon be executed. It hardly seems that things are going well for this new movement.

But perhaps we're missing the point. Almost every divine intervention in the Scriptures comes at a time of chaos or in the midst of suffering. From the moment of creation in the book of Genesis when God enters the darkness of the abyss to bring light, to the final notes of the book of Revelation when God promises victory to the persecuted church, we discover that God is always at work in the world.

God's kingdom is not reserved for the afterlife but breaks into the now. We need only ask for the eyes to see and the heart to embrace a kingdom that brings life out of suffering, now and always.

Meditation: The kingdom of God is best viewed from the bottom up. In other words, stripped of our usual securities as Jesus was in the desert, we learn to rely on God's mercy and surrender to God's priorities. Our own deserts may appear in the form of job insecurity or decline in physical or emotional health. How might God be using these times to strengthen and console us?

Prayer: Grant me, O God, the ability to see evidence of your kingdom in the ordinary rhythms of daily living. When chaos threatens, remind me that you are near.

February 19: Monday of the First Week of Lent

Living a Holy Life

Readings: Lev 19:1-2, 11-18; Matt 25:31-46

Scripture:
". . . Be holy, for I, the Lord, your God, am holy." (Lev 19:2)

Reflection: When I call to mind the people in my life who exude holiness, I find that not a single one of them is a perfect person. One could stand to be a little more gregarious, another could use a dose of moderation, and still another could be a little more prepared for upcoming events. Each one of them is flawed and each a sinner, and that gives me great comfort.

When I was young, I somehow picked up the idea that the saints were models of holiness because they were just shy of perfection and their moral character was blameless. Imagine my surprise, and relief, to learn that many of the saints in our tradition exhibited their fair share of flaws and quirks.

Human flaws and weaknesses do not diminish holiness. To be holy means to be called out for divine purposes. Our first reading from Leviticus describes what holiness looks like by way of the negative: not stealing or speaking falsely about others, not defrauding friends or employees, not judging others dishonestly or with partiality, not hating or taking revenge on others.

By way of the positive, being holy is loving our neighbor as we love ourselves. The parable of the sheep and goats in today's reading from the Gospel of Matthew reinforces this lesson. Those who are righteous (in right relationship with God, or holy) are those who feed the hungry, give drink to the thirsty, welcome the stranger, clothe the naked, care for the sick, and visit the imprisoned. Jesus goes so far as to say that such acts of loving service for others are in fact a way of loving him.

Meditation: The Scriptures tell us that being holy is about our cooperation with God's grace, not just for ourselves but for the sake of others with whom we are joined in Christ. There is no escaping the reality that our shared humanity is a pathway to holiness. Will we choose this path?

Prayer: Holy God, you invite us to mirror your concern and care for the neglected. Continue to work in our hearts so our actions are a product of your grace.

February 20: Tuesday of the First Week of Lent

Because I Said So

Readings: Isa 55:10-11; Matt 6:7-15

Scripture:
. . . [My word] shall not return to me void,
   but shall do my will,
   achieving the end for which I sent it. (Isa 55:11)

Reflection: I loved the neighborhood where I grew up. We were like one big extended family. We entered each other's homes freely, shared meals and chores together, played games and celebrated birthdays. I knew who my parents were, but I also knew the other parents could and would pitch in with hugs or discipline or teasing. They also shared in common the dreaded response to our sometimes whiney questions about why we had to do something we didn't want to do: "Because I said so." Those four words have a lot of power! Granted, they were usually spoken to close the discussion when our parents were weary of explaining their reasons, but those words had the capacity to make us complete a task.

While our readings today do not carry with them the exasperation of a tired parent, they do tell us about the power of words, particularly God's word. From Isaiah, we hear God's encouragement to a people in exile. Almost two generations passed with a large portion of Judah's population living in exile under Babylonian captivity. But the end of their separation from Jerusalem was coming to an end. They needed to believe that God had not abandoned them. When the people wonder if their time of exile is ending, the prophet basically says, "Yes, because God says so." God's word will achieve the end for which God sends it.

Centuries later, when Jesus teaches his followers how to pray, he invites us to trust that God's word is still the agent of God's will. When we pray for God's will to be done on earth as it is in heaven, when we pray for daily sustenance and for the ability to forgive, we are joining our voices with centuries of people who have also believed that these things will be done "because God says so."

Meditation: When God speaks, the words are not just *in*formative, they are *form*ative and *perform*ative. That means that we not only learn about God, but our hearts are formed so that we are more attuned to listening, and our actions are shaped by God's grace so that God's will may be done.

Prayer: Our Father, may your will be done in me, and may our faith communities know the power of your voice.

February 21: Wednesday of the First Week of Lent

The Way of Humility

Readings: Jonah 3:1-10; Luke 11:29-32

Scripture:
[A] heart contrite and humbled, O God, you will not spurn. (Ps 51:19)

Reflection: Recently, a dear friend died, and in the course of the days and weeks following his death, I kept seeing and hearing the word "humble" in people's remembrances of him. He was a brilliant scholar, an effective teacher, an accomplished writer and speaker, and he could be quite funny. In short, he was not humble in the way the word is sometimes used. He was not weak nor unassertive; he did not suffer from low self-esteem.

My friend was humble in the best sense of the word. He knew his shortcomings as well as his strengths. He sought wisdom from others without worrying about his ego. He took seriously his work and ministry without making himself the center of attention. In fact, his goal was to reflect Christ rather than hold a mirror to himself.

In today's readings, the virtue of humility calls for our attention. If you are familiar with the story of Jonah, you know the only reason he ended up in the belly of a big fish is that he was avoiding God's call. He was too prideful to heed God's command to preach to the inhabitants of Nineveh, believing they deserved destruction and were not worthy of a call to repentance. His "fishing" experience gave him a chance to repent of his own pride and do what God had asked of him: offer repentance to an enemy people.

The psalmist begs for a clean heart and a steadfast spirit, knowing that any way but the path of true humility will not lead to God. Jesus embodies the way of humility by becoming one of us and walking with us. Every day he offers each of us the opportunity to repent and discover this humble way as well.

Meditation: When we stumble on our own egos, believing we know a better way than God's way, we hurt ourselves and deprive others of the opportunity to encounter God who dwells in us. Where are we being called to humility?

Prayer: Teach us, O God, to value the opportunities to grow in humility so our egos do not get in the way of your will.

February 22: The Chair of Saint Peter the Apostle

Bearing Witness to Jesus, the Christ

Readings: 1 Pet 5:1-4; Matt 16:13-19

Scripture:
. . . "But who do you say that I am?" (Matt 16:15)

Reflection: For a number of years, I was involved in the Christian initiation process in my parish. I discovered that most adults who were inquiring about the faith found themselves in the process because of a personal connection to others. "I'm here because my neighbors are consistently living out their faith, and I want to understand what they have." "I'm interested in exploring more about faith because my children go to this parish school, and I'm impressed with their experience." "When my house was damaged by severe storms, it was people from this parish who arrived to help. I'm just curious."

The experience of another person's faith is often essential in building our own relationship with Christ. However, when all is said and done, our personal understanding of Christ and our relationship with Christ must be just that—our own. At some point along the way, we have to step into the scene that is described in our Gospel today. We need to move from reporting what others say and believe, even what others have experienced, and claim what *we* know to be true.

In today's Gospel, Jesus asks his disciples to speak for themselves and not simply report the speculation and ruminations of others. He is not testing them but rather is inviting them to move into a deeper understanding and relationship with him. In response, Peter speaks up and proclaims, "You are the Christ, the Son of the living God." Jesus invites us to do the same, to move from disinterested reporter to invested witness.

Meditation: Those in leadership in the church are tasked with helping members of their communities encounter Christ in a personal way, modeling how to bear witness to this essential relationship. When has the example of a leader in your local faith community helped you ponder some new aspect of your understanding of Christ and the Gospel?

Prayer: Give us, Christ, the opportunity to know you in a profoundly real way in our own lives. Ask us the hard questions, and then give us the courage to bear witness to you in word and deed.

February 22: The Chair of Saint Peter the Apostle

February 23: Friday of the First Week of Lent

The Dangers of Hypocrisy

Readings: Ezek 18:21-28; Matt 5:20-26

Scripture:
"[L]eave your gift there at the altar, go first and be reconciled . . ." (Matt 5:24)

Reflection: Among the reasons people offer for their estrangement from the church, one in particular rises to the surface: hypocrisy. Perhaps we who identify ourselves as followers of Christ don't "walk the talk" or are shortsighted about our own shortcomings. Goodness knows we can find plenty of examples of scandal and imperfection. Admittedly, we are a sinful people, but that does not release us from accountability.

The scandal of hypocrisy may receive more of Jesus' attention than any other behavior. He identifies it in his own religious community, calling out scribes and Pharisees for their shallow piety when appropriate, chastising his disciples for feigning scandal over wasteful expenditures, warning against claiming to love God while neglecting a neighbor, and lamenting that some find it easier to identify the sin in others than the sin in themselves.

What is hypocrisy but the failure to see the connection between what we claim to believe and how we actually act? Today's readings from the prophet Isaiah and the Gospel of

Matthew remind us that it is impossible to approach God if we have failed to repent of our own sin or do the hard work of reconciling with those we have wronged or who have wronged us.

It is God's desire that we live in such a way that our inner and outer worlds reflect one another. And it is God's gift of grace that enables us to take up the task of making peace between those parts of ourselves that are often at war with each other.

Meditation: The psalmist reminds us in today's responsorial psalm that God does not keep a tally of our sins but offers forgiveness to those who acknowledge their need for God's mercy. How can our experiences of God's mercy and reconciliation with others serve to heal the wounds left by hypocrisy?

Prayer: O God, when we desire to be seen as holy, remind us that true holiness comes from wholeness: reconciling ourselves with you and others, and living in a way that both our inner and outer worlds reflect your goodness.

February 24: Saturday of the First Week of Lent

Wholeness and Perfection

Readings: Deut 26:16-19; Matt 5:43-48

Scripture:
"[B]e perfect, just as your heavenly Father is perfect." (Matt 5:48)

Reflection: I can't help but wonder if a misguided drive for perfection is behind the great interest and investment in cosmetic surgery. It seems that every era has its definition of ideal beauty, and we are encouraged by a flurry of advertising and social media to believe we can attain bodily perfection if we invest in the right products or find the right surgeon. It can be overwhelming and frustrating when the ideal is not achieved.

Mind you, that's a superficial example, but I wonder if this interest in perfection bleeds over into the spiritual realm. Do we find ourselves holding up a particular ideal of what a good Christian looks like, and then become frustrated when that ideal is not achievable? Can we attain sinless perfection, or is that even what Jesus is talking about in today's Gospel?

It would be a mistake to assume that our twenty-first century understanding of perfection is what is intended in this passage from Matthew. In fact, the Greek word *teleios*, translated as "perfect," means mature, whole, or complete.

It is also important to acknowledge that this saying of Jesus is situated within the Sermon on the Mount in a section about loving one's enemies. That level of love requires a great depth of maturity in one's faith and a complete trust in God's grace in our lives. It requires for most of us a lifetime of working toward making whole what has been broken and bringing to maturity the seeds of mercy that God has planted.

Meditation: Today's first reading and psalm hold up the virtue of observing God's commands as a thoughtful response to God's love. Such obedience has the power to create the habits of heart that lead us to the wholeness God desires for us. Are we careful not to fall into the trap of strict obedience to God's law at the cost of obedience that is transforming?

Prayer: O God, we seek you with all our being, knowing you have shaped our hearts for right relationship with you. Bless our efforts with the grace to grow in maturity as we bear witness to you.

February 25: Second Sunday of Lent

Listening to the Lord

Readings: Gen 22:1-2, 9a, 10-13, 15-18; Rom 8:31b-34; Mark 9:2-10

Scripture:
. . . "This is my beloved Son. Listen to him." (Mark 9:7)

Reflection: "You're not listening to me." How many times have we heard or said these words in the midst of a discussion? Usually there is some exasperation or weariness behind them. Why is it that we are able to hear but fail to listen?

Hearing is the process of receiving sound, and for most of us it is a rather passive process. We use hearing to gather information, and some of that information can elicit an emotional response. Listening, on the other hand, is far from passive. It requires real attention, curiosity, and empathy. When we are actively listening, we are in the process of assigning meaning to what we are hearing. Little wonder that St. Benedict begins his rule of life with the words, "Listen with the ear of your hearts." This type of listening increases our ability to think and imagine, to engage our moral will and shape our dreams.

In today's Gospel, Peter, James, and John are on a mountaintop where they experience a revelation of Jesus in his glorified state. He is transfigured before them, and the voice of God instructs them to listen to his Son. Of course, they have heard Jesus speak countless times by this point in their journeys with him, but have they fully understood him? Have the disciples engaged their hearts so they would not merely be "wowed" by what they saw and heard but transformed by who he is and who he calls them to be?

Listening to Jesus will transform his followers in every age.

Meditation: In what ways am I creating the time and space to *listen* to (not just *hear*) the voice of Jesus? In my prayer and study of God's word, am I challenged by his teaching? Energized by his vision of the kingdom of God? More committed to living differently?

Prayer: Jesus, beloved Son of God, condition my heart to listen intently for your voice. Draw me into your vision of the victory of life over death.

February 26: Monday of the Second Week of Lent

Managing Our Expectations

Readings: Dan 9:4b-10; Luke 6:36-38

Scripture:
"Be merciful, just as your Father is merciful.
"Stop judging and you will not be judged." (Luke 6:36-37)

Reflection: The adult child of a friend of mine says he's given up on Christianity because it's all about laws and not about love or mercy. He's disillusioned by Christians who are busy passing judgment on the behavior of others while not attending to their own sin. Either we've done a poor job of upholding the Gospel or he's not paying attention to the breadth and depth of our tradition and practices. Or maybe it's a little of both.

Our Gospel today urges a goodly measure of self-examination. If we are honest with ourselves, we are aware of personal behaviors and attitudes that are an affront to God's commands. We covet what we do not or cannot have; we do harm to others through gossip; we allow the false gods of status and power to corrupt our relationship with God. And if we are even more honest, were it not for God's completely unmerited mercy, we would have no hope of living differently, no hope of seeing ourselves as God sees us.

It is a beautiful thing to know that we can come before God to simply and honestly admit who we are. If we expect judgment, we will instead find that God's justice is always accompanied by divine mercy. If we expect condemnation, we will instead find freedom. If we expect isolation, we will instead receive an invitation to share in God's love.

When the experience of honesty, compassion, forgiveness, and restoration becomes the hallmark of our identity as Christians, the measure of mercy we show to others will be authentic.

Meditation: Dominican Timothy Radcliffe says, "For Christians, the great lie is to see other people unmercifully, to shut our eyes to the goodness of their humanity and to weight them down with the burden of their sins." Who among us wants to be judged and remembered by the worst thing we've ever done?

Prayer: May my experience of your mercy, O loving God, translate into compassion for others. Give me the wisdom and insight to see others as you mercifully see me.

February 27: Tuesday of the Second Week of Lent

The Value of Prophets

Readings: Isa 1:10, 16-20; Matt 23:1-12

Scripture:
Make justice your aim: redress the wronged,
  hear the orphan's plea, defend the widow. (Isa 1:17)

Reflection: I knew a priest who made everyone uncomfortable and at the same time inspired them. I'll call him Fr. Joe. He had this uncanny way of speaking the truth in situations where most people would have kept their mouths shut until a later or more private time. Fr. Joe was not trying to be obnoxious or awkward; he was so steeped in the social teachings of the church that he could not help but speak for those who were not "at the table." Some of his speaking was with words, and sometimes he spoke through his actions.

Fr. Joe was cut from the prophetic mold we find in Scripture, and we know God's prophets are never the most popular folks in the world. A prophet holds up the mirror of God's covenant with us and demands that we see the truth of how we are (or are not) living the covenant in the real world. Are we in right relationship with God and others? Are we committed to justice for the oppressed and forgotten? Are we living in the way of mercy?

Today, Isaiah speaks to his fellow Israelites and to us when he says to make justice our aim. Further, he promises that those who are willing to obey God's commands will be transformed. Jesus also calls forth a way of life that removes the heavy burdens of blind obedience. He chastises religious leaders who do not live as they preach, knowing their roles can either disillusion the faithful or provide examples to follow.

Meditation: Thank God for the prophets among us, those who are committed to God's call to care for the poor, live with mercy, and give voice to those who are forgotten. The church is always in danger of becoming a closed circle or more of a club than the living Body of Christ. Where does your own community need to be stretched in this regard?

Prayer: May your words, O Lord, abide in our hearts so that we see the dignity of each person, recognize their worth, and create communities that are just and merciful.

February 28: Wednesday of the Second Week of Lent

The Heart of a Servant

Readings: Jer 18:18-20; Matt 20:17-28

Scripture:
"[W]hoever wishes to be great among you shall be your servant . . ." (Matt 20:26)

Reflection: I used to say jokingly that if you plan to work for the church, be prepared to take on several occupations you may not have bargained for: dishwasher, teacher, counselor, janitor, driver, and head of the complaints department. Most parishes have more needs than personnel to meet those needs, and more idea-generators than idea-doers. And maybe that's not a bad thing, at least if we learn the art of balance. It gives us instant training in being servants and opens up opportunities to shape patterns of service that can greatly enrich our lives.

A mature understanding of service helps us recognize the dignity of work and the dignity of the human person. My work, whether it is cleaning the parish kitchen after an event or presenting a faith formation session, allows me to use my gifts to serve others' needs. It puts me in touch with the people who populate the pews of my parish and helps me see Christ in them and focus on what they need. Nourishing a servant's heart can move each of us from self-indulgence to self-giving, and can connect us in an intimate way with the Body of Christ in our midst.

Just as importantly, mature servants know not to imagine themselves as quasi-saviors. When we strive to live with hearts of true service, we recognize the gifts that are present in those we serve, and we look for opportunities to call forth those gifts. Not only does this benefit each of us, but it creates communities reflective of the service Jesus models for us.

Meditation: Jesus' instruction that the greatest will be servants comes just after the mother of two of his disciples asks that her sons be seated in places of honor in the kingdom Jesus has been revealing. This note of tone-deafness reminds us to listen closely not only to what Jesus says but to pay attention to those whom he serves with the very gift of his life.

Prayer: Jesus, servant to those who seem to be least among us, stoke the desire in us to imitate your commitment to give of yourself for the sake of others.

February 29: Thursday of the Second Week of Lent

Sometimes the Truth Stings

Readings: Jer 17:5-10; Luke 16:19-31

Scripture:
". . . 'If they will not listen to Moses and the prophets, neither will they be persuaded if someone should rise from the dead.'" (Luke 16:31)

Reflection: Who doesn't love a good reversal-of-fortune story? We want the struggling team to upset the stars of field and arena, the secretary to get the better of an abusive or incompetent boss, and the day laborer to one day own the farm. It satisfies something in us if we empathize with the underdog who then becomes the "big dog." But what if we discover that we are on the opposite end of that equation? If we're already the "big dog," we might wince a bit in the telling or hearing of these stories.

Today's Gospel is a reversal-of-fortune story. A rich man ignores the plight of a homeless man named Lazarus who lies sick at his door. When Lazarus dies, he is rewarded by being taken to the bosom of Abraham (a figurative way of expressing intimacy with God even after death). When the rich man dies, he is banished to the netherworld. In a further insult, even in death and suffering, the rich man begs that Lazarus bring water to quench his thirst. Failing that, couldn't Lazarus be sent to warn the rich man's family? In truth, even in his desperation, the rich man does not see the humanity of Lazarus, and still does not understand that the key to living a blessed life is not some hidden secret.

Surely we feel the sting of this story, not just as individuals but as a culture and a nation, where there is often a great divide between the "haves" and "have-nots." We may feel a similar sting when we read in this same Gospel the Canticle of Mary as she praises God who fills the hungry with good things and sends the rich away empty (1:53), or when we hear Jesus read from the prophet Isaiah saying his mission is to bring glad tidings to the poor (4:18).

Will we let this "sting" change our hearts?

Meditation: Let's be careful not to dismiss the lesson of today's Gospel. When so many people in our world live in the misery of poverty, isolation, and neglect, we have the distinct obligation to do as Christ would do: bring glad tidings, provide comfort, and invite the neglected to the table that has so generously served us.

Prayer: O Lord, help us to draw from the well of your generosity, giving without measure in ways that effect positive change in the lives of our brothers and sisters.

February 29: Thursday of the Second Week of Lent

March 1: Friday of the Second Week of Lent

Embracing the Dream

Readings: Gen 37:3-4, 12-13a, 17b-28a; Matt 21:33-43, 45-46

Scripture:
. . . "Here comes that master dreamer! Come on, let us kill him . . ." (Gen 37:19-20)

Reflection: August of 1930, August of 1963, July of 1969 and 1972, October of 2012. These dates are associated with just some of the dreamers in our lifetimes who faced misunderstanding, opposition, and attempts (some successful) on their lives. Mahatma Gandhi of India, Martin Luther King, Jr., of the United States, Steve Biko of South Africa, and Malala Yousafzai of Pakistan, all carried within them dreams that were not just personal aspirations, but dreams of a world where all people's dignity is honored. They were not the first, nor will they be the last, whose dreams put them in harm's way.

What is it that makes us suspicious of people who dare to dream? Is it that they do not seem to honor the status quo? Do their dreams challenge us to let go of dearly held values of our own? Is there jealousy involved? Fear?

Today in our story from Genesis we meet Joseph, the youngest and favorite son of Jacob. When his dreams upset the presumed order of honor and privilege in their family, his brothers sell him into slavery (though they initially plan to kill him). Later, after Joseph has risen to a level of power in Pharaoh's administration, he is able to save his family from famine and certain death. The boy his brothers once eyed with jealousy is generous and forgiving. The brothers' fears and envy were misplaced. Did they learn a lesson? Will we?

Meditation: The "dream" of Jesus is the kingdom of God. This is not fantasy but a roadmap of a future where slave and free, woman and man, sinner and saint can sit at the same table and be nourished by God's truth. Are we willing to allow our hearts and our behaviors to be shaped by such a dream? Will we protect this dream as we work toward making it a reality?

Prayer: Gift us, O God, with the wisdom to dream the dream of Jesus. Calm our fears as we discern how you are speaking in our world today. Put aside our prejudices so we can recognize where you are at work.

March 2: Saturday of the Second Week of Lent

Living in the Moment

Readings: Mic 7:14-15, 18-20; Luke 15:1-3, 11-32

Scripture:
" 'But now we must celebrate and rejoice, because your brother was dead and has come to life again . . .' " (Luke 15:32)

Reflection: The story of the generous father and two sons, one dutiful and one reckless, is so familiar that we may hear it rather passively and miss its many insights. Today, let's pay close attention and explore a small but significant word in its final verse: *now. This* is the time that "we must celebrate and rejoice."

Have you ever noticed how seldom we are in tune with the significance of a moment, how often we miss living in the now? Like the older of the two sons, we may fail to recognize the magnitude of a moment because we are living in the past or are caught up in the perceived unfairness of a situation. We can become trapped in measuring our own worth, and in the process, fail to see that God's goodness has nothing to do with what we merit. We might also trap others in their character flaws and sinfulness, not allowing them to evolve and plot out a new future for themselves.

Part of a healthy spirituality is living in the present moment so we can open ourselves to its treasures. The father in our parable invites his older son to take off his blinders.

There will be time enough to work out the details of accepting his brother's return; now is the time to celebrate. Now is the time to recognize a new opportunity, a new lease on life, not just for the younger son but for all three characters as they make their way back to each other.

Meditation: When has a moment filled with meaning missed your attention? When has a preoccupation with past behavior prevented you from seeing in yourself or others the treasure of transformation and new life? Commit yourself to attending to the now, the moment in which we live and breathe, the moment that calls for a response.

Prayer: God of all time, help us to surrender the past to your mercy and the future to your wisdom. Meet us in the now and encourage us to stay there, responding with full attention to what you are doing in our midst.

March 3: Third Sunday of Lent

Obedience in Love

Readings: Exod 20:1-17; 1 Cor 1:22-25; John 2:13-25

Scripture:
"I, the LORD am your God, who brought you out of the land of Egypt, that place of slavery." (Exod 20:2)

Reflection: A bit of popular wisdom proposes that many atrocities in our world are committed not by breaking the rules but by blindly following them. Let's consider how this insight might relate to today's readings.

At times we all fall into the rut of thinking of the Ten Commandments as a list of "Thou shalt nots," rendering them in a way that makes God's law feel like a burden to be carried rather than a way of living that is fruitful. But if we focus on the line just before the listing of God's commands, the entire enterprise of obedience is rightly reframed: "I, the LORD am your God, who brought you out of the land of Egypt, that place of slavery" (Exod 20:2).

Before uttering a single command to the Hebrew people, God first invites them to recall who delivered them from slavery. God is the one who freed them from oppression to experience freedom. God is the one who knows their pain and wants to shape them into a people who are fully aware of their dignity. The law given to Moses is not commanded by some despot anxious to oppress them further; this law is a gift from their Creator and Redeemer. Across the centuries, like our ancestors in faith, we discover that obedience to God's law is a loving response to the God who loves us first and best.

God, our Creator, knows that love truly sets us free, and the Ten Commandments help us live the practical implications of loving both God and neighbor. Keeping the Sabbath and calling upon the Lord's name creates worship as a core habit of our hearts. Protecting life, honoring the relationships and property of others, speaking truthfully and lovingly, and refusing to give in to envy, all create the heart habit of recognizing the dignity of others and the need for community.

Meditation: The psalmist reminds us that God's law refreshes the soul and is trustworthy because God is trustworthy. Does our obedience feel burdensome, or does it invite others to experience God as we have?

Prayer: O Giver of the law, help us to remove the blinders that prevent us from seeing you as the author of all that is good and worthy of our loving obedience.

March 4: Monday of the Third Week of Lent

Resistance to the Prophet

Readings: 2 Kgs 5:1-15b; Luke 4:24-30

Scripture:
"[N]o prophet is accepted in his own native place." (Luke 4:24)

Reflection: The verse above from today's Gospel could be read as "familiarity breeds contempt" in the sense that we may not always appreciate what is right in our midst. The neighbor whose dog drives us crazy but who shares his fabulous baking is not truly appreciated until he moves away. The doctor who can be abrupt but who always fits us in when we are in need suddenly retires, and only then do we understand how blessed we were. Today's Gospel, however, is not simply about missing something or someone when it's too late.

Prophets are not fortune-tellers; the only future they predict is the one associated with fidelity or infidelity to God's law. They offer contemporary critique of the attitudes and values of their times, critique that is not always well-received. In the Gospel of Luke, Jesus begins his ministry by reading from the prophet Isaiah, proclaiming that Isaiah's message of glad tidings to the poor, liberty to captives, recovery of sight to the blind, and freedom for the oppressed has come to fulfillment in him.

At first the people speak favorably of him, but the situation turns sour when Jesus references events in Israel's past when only a few heeded the prophets Elijah and Elisha. The people quickly realize that Jesus is indicting those who have failed to respond to him as well. Resistance to change, fear of losing control, and the inability to allow God to act in fresh ways are all part of their soured response to Jesus.

Clearly the verse from today's Gospel has a deeper meaning: those who wish to follow Jesus must invest themselves in a new vision of reality rather than fearing what they have to lose.

Meditation: In his prophetic role, Jesus calls for a level of fidelity that will turn the world upside down. Are we ready for this ride of a lifetime?

Prayer: Jesus, bringer of God's kingdom, when our impulse is to flee in the face of your commands, give us staying power. When our impulse is to defend the status quo, make us pliable. When we feel threatened by what we may lose, remind us of all we have to gain by following you. Open our hearts to give you a welcoming home.

March 5: Tuesday of the Third Week of Lent

Refreshed by Forgiveness

Readings: Dan 3:25, 34-43; Matt 18:21-35

Scripture:
. . . "Lord, if my brother sins against me, how often must I forgive him? As many as seven times?" (Matt 18:21)

Reflection: It is amazing how often the Gospels return to the theme of forgiveness—the need for it, the experience of it, and the transformation it offers to each of us. It's like sitting at the water's edge and feeling the lapping of refreshment that calls us further into the cool water on a hot day. We long for waters that will cool the heat of arguments and wash clean the remains of bitterness and resentment. We want the hard edges of our hearts to be buffed smooth.

We need to be reminded that there is a better way. And so, Jesus repeatedly takes us by the hand into the deeper waters of forgiveness where we might find our hearts refreshed, and where the harshness within and around us can be rinsed away. The more we visit these waters, the more comfortable we will be as we learn to navigate them.

In today's Gospel, Peter asks Jesus if he must forgive someone seven times. I picture him feeling awfully proud of himself since he surely knows the number seven is symbolic of fullness or completeness. Jesus, however, invites Peter deeper by replying that forgiveness should be given seventy-seven times! God's forgiveness is infinite, lavishly generous, and when we live with this knowledge and experience, we become capable of imitating what we have received. Perhaps this is one way of understanding grace: God's capacity for lavish generosity being awakened in us.

Meditation: Have you ever watched someone plunge into cool waters and then resurface? Their eyes are wide, their heart is pounding, and their skin is tingling with alertness. Have you felt this sensation yourself? Experiencing forgiveness is a bit like this if we pay attention. Whether giving mercy or receiving it, we feel a little more alive to the possibility of a different world, a world pulsing with generosity of heart.

Prayer: You, O God, know the burdens we carry as well as those we inflict on others. Help us to leave at the water's edge whatever weighs us down, and then lead us to take the plunge into the sea of forgiveness. Let us seek your grace to become a forgiving people.

March 6: Wednesday of the Third Week of Lent

The Power of Memory

Readings: Deut 4:1, 5-9; Matt 5:17-19

Scripture:
"[B]e earnestly on your guard not to forget the things which your own eyes have seen, nor let them slip from your memory as long as you live, but teach them to your children and to your children's children." (Deut 4:9)

Reflection: Caring for a loved one with dementia reinforces how essential memory is to being human. More than simply retrieving information stored over a lifetime, memory includes events and people as well as the feelings that accompany them; it determines how we see ourselves and our world. One of the reasons loss of memory through dementia is so devastating is that the person we once knew seems to slowly but surely slip away. One of our sacred tasks as caregivers is to preserve the memory of who those in our care truly are in their totality, not just who they are while experiencing dementia.

Today's readings from Deuteronomy and Matthew evoke the importance of memory and the danger of what we might call "spiritual dementia" or "spiritual amnesia." When Moses delivers God's law to the Hebrew people, he reminds them that when they honor the law, they give testimony about God to the surrounding nations. He urges them "not to forget," and by that he means that they are to remember not only God's commands but also what they have experienced, knowing God as they do. In the Gospel, Jesus wants his followers to see in him the fulfillment of God's commands. Jesus never forgets who he is and *whose* he is, and he desires the same for all of us.

Our sacramental life, the proclamation of the Scriptures, our personal prayer, and our public worship all serve as tools of sacred memory. Through them we continually remember what God has done *for* us and continues to do *in* us.

Meditation: At the core of who we are, God is present, stirring in us the capacity to tell and retell the stories of what God has done for us. When we share our sacred memories, we are engaging in a deeply human task. When have you been bolstered by another person's sharing of faith? When has your ongoing memory of God at work in you been a source of care for another person?

Prayer: Your commands, O God, give us the opportunity to respond to your generous love. They shape who we are and what we bring to our world. Give us the constancy of remembering how to be just and loving and merciful.

March 7: Thursday of the Third Week of Lent

Softening Hard Hearts

Readings: Jer 7:23-28; Luke 11:14-23

Scripture:
If today you hear his voice, harden not your hearts. (Ps 95:8)

Reflection: Why in the world would we harden our hearts upon hearing God's voice? And yet, this must be a common phenomenon because the Scriptures reference hardness of heart, stony hearts, or unrepentant hearts at least one hundred times. Are we afraid of God? Or afraid of being softhearted?

The world teaches us that success requires us to be tough, cunning, and laser-focused; in short, to be hardened. To be fair, the Scriptures contain some of the same lessons using slightly different terms. We are urged to stand firm, to be as shrewd as serpents, and to be single-hearted. So, what's the difference? The focus and condition of our hearts.

The biblical tradition urges us to be tough in the face of evil and stand firm in the face of suffering (Phil 1:27; 1 Pet 5:9), to be shrewd or cunning in the face of danger or opposition (Matt 10:16), and to be single-hearted in or laser-focused on our devotion to God (Ps 86:11; Matt 6:24). Our ultimate goal as Christians is not success as it is usually measured, but living in a way that makes us pliable and receptive to God's voice speaking to our hearts.

When God speaks words of comfort and mercy, we are usually receptive. But God's words of correction are hard to accept. Harder still is hearing the voice of God that turns our world upside down, challenging our values or taking blinders off our eyes so that we see suffering and oppression as God sees it. Resistance to God's voice hardens our hearts, robbing us of our full humanity and the potential to offer the world what it desperately needs.

Meditation: Hardness of heart goes hand in hand with pride, or thinking of ourselves as the arbiters of truth and the masters of our own destinies. A healthy dose of humility allows us to listen for God's voice more intently and to freely dismantle the hardened walls around our hearts. Are we open to the grace of a supple heart?

Prayer: Give us discerning hearts, O God, so we may learn to recognize your voice in the midst of so many other messages. Give us humility to recognize that you alone speak words that set our hearts free to love.

March 7: Thursday of the Third Week of Lent

March 8: Friday of the Third Week of Lent

False Securities

Readings: Hos 14:2-10; Mark 12:28-34

Scripture:
"Assyria will not save us . . ." (Hos 14:4)

Reflection: At the time of the prophet Hosea, the northern kingdom of Israel was in a state of disarray. Several of its kings had been assassinated, and their once prosperous and stable nation was embroiled in political chaos. At the same time the larger empires of Egypt and Assyria were flexing their muscles. In the end, shortly after the time of Hosea, Israel fell to Assyria, the very nation they hoped would protect them.

It is understandable that a small nation would feel insecure when greater powers are surrounding them, gobbling up other small states along the way. Naturally, they formed alliances hoping for protection. But God's prophets wanted Israel to know that such military and political pacts provided little more than a false sense of security. History shows that even the firmest pacts are subject to the winds of change.

While we live in a different time and place than our ancient ancestors, the desire to construct walls of security around ourselves is universal. Nations, organizations, families, and individuals naturally yearn to feel safe in their surroundings and have the obligation to defend the defenseless. But today's warning from Hosea is a reminder that we cannot put our ultimate trust in anything but God's sustaining presence with us. It is God's kingdom that is enduring; it is God's covenant that is true and firm; it is God's call for fidelity and love of neighbor that provides true security.

Meditation: In many nations around the world, there is growing polarization between political parties, between haves and have-nots, and even within our communities of faith. There is a tendency to find a place of seeming security for our own values and ideas. But when we attach ourselves so firmly to one set of ideas or to one particular group, we may miss the opportunity to occasionally reevaluate and see where God is leading or how God may be asking us to name and move beyond our fears. When have you discovered a need to reorient yourself to the true security of God?

Prayer: We rely on your love, O Lord, but still find ourselves hedging our bets, attaching ourselves to systems of power and sources of security that are fleeting. Give us single-hearted devotion to you and direct our ways.

March 9: Saturday of the Third Week of Lent

Know Thyself

Readings: Hos 6:1-6, Luke 18:9-14

Scripture:
". . . 'O God, be merciful to me a sinner.'" (Luke 18:13)

Reflection: You've probably had the experience of taking a personality test or personality inventory at some point in your life. Typically these inventories ask a series of questions and then draw conclusions about our personalities, or they focus on personality categories in order to help us identify our personality type. Ironically, most people who use these tools for self-discovery will tell you that they find themselves assigning a personality type to their spouse, friend, or sibling long before they recognize where they might find themselves!

I couldn't help but think of the experience of using a personality inventory when hearing today's Gospel that places a Pharisee and a tax collector in the temple area. Both men are engaged in prayer, certainly a good thing, but each man approaches it differently. The Pharisee talks to God not so much about himself as about the other man. The Pharisee finds it easier to analyze the other rather than himself, a bit like putting the tax collector in what he believes is the proper slot in the inventory of personalities. The tax collector, however, is searching within himself, offering to God what he finds. He is not concerned with evaluating the condition of someone else nearly as much as he is with understanding his own condition, a spiritual exercise that leads him to ask for mercy.

Meditation: Pope Francis reminds us that the Latin root for "mercy" means to open one's heart to wretchedness. But we do not wallow in that self-realization. Rather, we take our condition to the Lord who gives himself to us, accepts us, and then bows down to forgive us. Wonder of wonders, we are invited into this most intimate expression of love. Has such an experience of mercy ever left you in awe of God's compassion?

Prayer: Lord of Mercy, help us to know that our identity as sinners does not define us nearly as much as your identity as Love itself. Show us your mercy, draw us into your loving embrace, and we shall be made new.

March 10: Fourth Sunday of Lent

God's Will to Save Us

Readings: 2 Chr 36:14-16, 19-23; Eph 2:4-10; John 3:14-21

Scripture:
For God did not send his Son into the world to condemn the world, but that the world might be saved through him. (John 3:17)

Reflection: We have grown accustomed to seeing posters and bumper stickers that simply say "John 3:16." This verse is a perfect thumbnail expression of the depth of God's love: "For God so loved the world that he gave his only Son . . ." As much as I treasure this truth, it's the next verse (John 3:17, above) that I believe we might need to hear most in an atmosphere that is often charged with images of a God who sits in harsh judgment and is ready to smite all enemies.

The reason God sends his Son is not for condemnation but for salvation. That is very good news because it tells us that God's intent for us is never destruction. Only we can be destructive of God's desires for us. The more we grow in the conviction that God intends salvation, the less likely we are to blame God for evil in the world or for the violence done in God's name.

What does Jesus' mission of salvation look like? A beautiful answer can be found later in this same Gospel when Jesus teaches about the good shepherd and his sheep. He says, "A thief comes only to steal and slaughter and destroy; I came so that they might have life and have it more abundantly" (John 10:10).

Salvation looks like abundant life, fullness of life, living in an awareness of being made in the image of God. In Jesus, we find the pattern for living abundantly: speaking truth in love, being a healing presence, offering mercy, standing with the oppressed, accompanying the outcast.

Meditation: In some circles, abundant life is equated with abundant possessions, somehow seen as a sign of God's blessing. Scripture offers a better approach: a way of being that is permeated with the grace to live generously whatever our circumstances. In this, we find our true calling and purpose and can savor the taste of salvation.

Prayer: God of all, may your work of salvation stir in us the grace to accept your mercy, the desire to love you more, and the will to share your love in practical ways. Your Son is a gift to a hurting world. May we offer the gift of his saving presence to all we meet.

March 11: Monday of the Fourth Week of Lent

Inhabiting the Stories of Jesus

Readings: Isa 65:17-21; John 4:43-54

Scripture:
. . . "Sir, come down before my child dies." Jesus said to him, "You may go; your son will live." (John 4:49-50)

Reflection: I have a friend who is a retired military officer. Bill was one of a group of participants, I among them, who attended a retreat offered by a gifted biblical storyteller. In the course of our days together, we were invited to discover the power of stories in general, and the stories of Jesus in particular. Toward the end of our time, we worked in small groups to "retell" a story from the Gospels, to bring it to life for all the participants in some new way.

Bill became the storyteller for his group, and I clearly recall the fresh perspective he brought to the story we hear in today's Gospel: the encounter between Jesus and the royal official from Capernaum. Bill and his group imagined the royal official as a military officer assigned to Capernaum by the Roman governor of the region. In other words, he was a representative of the foreign forces occupying Israel at the time of Jesus. He was used to giving orders, not taking them.

In Bill's telling of the story, the officer likely went to Jesus to heal his son, expecting that Jesus would obediently come back to Capernaum with him. In a kind of role reversal, Jesus became the one giving orders, telling the officer to return home where he would find his son healed.

This retelling rings true, in part because it reflects the historical realities of the region at the time. But in larger part, it rings true because it resonates deeply with Jesus' proclamation of the kingdom of God, a kingdom where anyone in need can come to Jesus, where national or religious affiliations are never barriers, and where healing is given priority over protocol.

Meditation: Review in your mind and heart some of your most treasured stories of Jesus interacting with people during his public ministry. Does one of these stories in particular speak to you during this Lenten season? Spend some time mulling over the characters and the dynamics of the scene to better appreciate the details and how they speak to you.

Prayer: Jesus, your encounters with people along the way always gave them a story to tell. Refresh my own story of encountering you.

March 12: Tuesday of the Fourth Week of Lent

Wanting What We Need

Readings: Ezek 47:1-9, 12; John 5:1-16

Scripture:
. . . "Do you want to be well?" (John 5:6)

Reflection: Do you ever feel stuck in a situation or in a mood, and you feel like there's no getting out of it? Or like you don't have the energy to even consider your options, much less the will to change what needs to be changed?

A toxic work environment, hurtful relationships, addictions, a chronic illness—any of these can feel like the quicksand we recall from old movies and cartoons, sucking us downward, leaving us barely able to call out for help. What stops us from seeking what we need, even if what we need is primarily a change of attitude? Sometimes we become so stuck that we forget to *want* what we truly *need*.

Today's Gospel account introduces us to a man, ill for thirty-eight years, who has been lying by the pool of Bethesda waiting for someone to help him into the healing waters. Perhaps the man was stuck in his situation for so long that he had to be reminded by Jesus of his purpose in being there: to be healed. But maybe we can look a little more deeply. If nothing else, this man has exhibited unwavering hope by consistently placing himself near the opportunity for healing. Perhaps, we can also acknowledge that his mere presence over such a long period of time should have prompted some kind soul to assist him.

But perhaps what is most important is that Jesus knows what the man needs even if the man doesn't know it himself. Urged to invest in his own healing process—to rise, take up his mat, and walk (perhaps even limping and uncertain at first)—his healing begins.

Meditation: Just as Jesus knows what this particular man needs and desires as he lies ill in Jerusalem, so does Jesus know what we need and desire. He asks us if we want to be healed, if we want to be forgiven, if we want to know joy. Let's begin by investing ourselves in what it takes to want what we need.

Prayer: Healer of all, help us to place before you the needs that fill our hearts, and give us the agility to walk the path of healing.

March 13: Wednesday of the Fourth Week of Lent

The Unity of Creation

Readings: Isa 49:8-15; John 5:17-30

Scripture:
Sing out, O heavens, and rejoice, O earth,
   break forth into song, you mountains.
For the Lord comforts his people
   and shows mercy to his afflicted. (Isa 49:13)

Reflection: Sometimes I wonder if we live in a bubble of our own making. We humans tend to believe that the world revolves around us, that as the crown of creation, made in the image of God, we have authority over all that the eye can see. Nature is used and sometimes abused to prosper us; after all, God gave humans dominion over all of creation in the first account of creation in Genesis.

But are we misinterpreting the meaning of "dominion" over creation? It is, after all, easier to focus on the benefits of creation for our use than on the responsibility we have as part of the created world. What benefits human beings should benefit all creation, and what benefits creation will hold blessings for human beings.

The Bible uses images from nature with great frequency. In today's reading from Isaiah, the gifts of nature are signs of restoration as Israel's time of exile comes to an end. In the psalm response, even nature rejoices when God's people experience divine comfort and mercy. And in the Gospel passage from John, the finality of death as part of the natural order of things will be overcome as we listen for and become obedient to the voice of the Son of God.

We do not exist in a bubble unto ourselves. We are part of God's creation. Our role as caregivers of creation reminds us that God promises not just new life for *us*, but an entirely new heaven and new earth.

Meditation: The prophet Isaiah offers words of encouragement to those in exile in Babylon. His words paint a beautiful scene, describing how the created world is anticipating their return to Jerusalem: pastureland is plentiful, the weather is cooperative, springs of water and roadways through mountains direct their travel, and even the mountains rejoice at their return. The stirring of Israel's collective imagination with these images from nature prepares their hearts to respond to God's tender care.

Prayer: God of creation, you have fashioned us to find in nature a bond that is both sturdy and fragile. May our sharing in the patterns of scarcity and abundance, dying and rising, turn our hearts to you.

March 14: Thursday of the Fourth Week of Lent

Struggling with Hard Passages

Readings: Exod 32:7-14; John 5:31-47

Scripture:
But Moses implored the LORD . . . (Exod 32:11)

Reflection: There are many passages of Scripture that puzzle me. Passages, for example, that speak of God's anger or vengeance are hard to reconcile with the countless times God is described as merciful and forgiving, even slow to anger.

Of course, any time we think we can fully comprehend God, we can be quite certain that we are not adequate to the task. I wonder how often even the biblical writers were projecting their own human nature onto God or were describing more of a symbolic reality about God rather than offering a literal description. Today's readings raise those questions for me again. In Exodus, for example, God is described as ready to consume his own people with anger at their worship of a golden calf.

There is something I do appreciate amid these types of passages, and that is the honest dialogue that often emerges. In this case, Moses stands as an intermediary between God and the Hebrew people who are weary of wandering in the desert and who appear to be safeguarding their chances of survival by erecting an image of another god. They are not yet ready to cast their lot entirely with the God of their liberation who is being less than direct in delivering them to the Promised Land. Moses, who is clearly and completely committed, asks God to relent, not merely to save the people, but to save the reputation of God as one who rescues and does not destroy his own. Such intimacy with God—and the honest dialogue it allows—is not reserved for Moses alone, but is available to each of us.

Meditation: What do we communicate about God by the ways we speak of God and to God? Are we willing to acknowledge that our relationship with God is always evolving, and that our questions can be an avenue to a deeper relationship?

Prayer: God of Mystery, keep us humble enough to know that we cannot control or contain you, and bold enough to know that you desire to be known.

March 15: Friday of the Fourth Week of Lent

Abandoning Preconceived Ideas

Readings: Wis 2:1a, 12-22; John 7:1-2, 10, 25-30

Scripture:
"But we know where he is from. When the Christ comes, no one will know where he is from." (John 7:27)

Reflection: In today's Gospel, Jesus is in Jerusalem for the feast of Tabernacles, one of the major Jewish feasts. Pilgrims from far and wide set up booths or tents for the week, celebrating God's abundance in the harvest as well as God's generosity in traveling with them in the wilderness after deliverance from slavery in Egypt. Jesus has kept a fairly low profile in John's Gospel up to this point, but now, amid his fellow Jews, his teaching and his presence draw the attention of many who wonder if he is the Messiah, the Christ.

Those who doubt that Jesus is the anointed of God point out what must have been an assumption at the time, that the Messiah would be an unknown, someone whose origins were not common knowledge. "We know his parents," some may have thought, or "Surely a boy who grew up in Nazareth is not the Messiah." These preconceptions prevent them from recognizing that the Messiah is in their midst in the person of Jesus.

While there is great value in knowing our religious traditions, sometimes we may have picked up a skewed understanding or are giving a high priority to some practice that is not central to our faith. We can end up locked into a particular way of anticipating how God works and miss the ways God actually is working. We may limit our ability to appreciate that God often moves among us in unexpected ways. After all, who would have thought a little boy from humble beginnings would be God's beloved Son?

Meditation: When have we stubbornly held on to immature beliefs or preconceived ideas about God? How often have our own well-worn ideas about religion stood in the way of having a vibrant experience of faith? Today we can invite God to help us abandon any preconceived ideas that stand in the way of recognizing how Christ is at work in our midst.

Prayer: God of surprises, in this season that leads us to your Son's cross and then to his empty tomb, remind us that your work among us might reveal some surprising insights. We open our hearts to what you have in store.

March 16: Saturday of the Fourth Week of Lent

Security in God's Call

Readings: Jer 11:18-20; John 7:40-53

Scripture:
Yet I, like a trusting lamb led to slaughter, had not realized they were hatching plots against me . . . (Jer 11:19)

Reflection: There's nothing quite like the feeling of having been betrayed. It cuts to the core of who we are to discover that someone we trust has proven to be unworthy of our trust. It might be a coworker or family member, a friend or neighbor; the severing of once-sturdy bonds causes us to question our own judgment and plants seeds of sorrow and fear that will only sicken us if we let them take root.

Among the prophets, Jeremiah is the most transparent about the personal cost of his ministry. In his writings we find six passages that serve as his "confessions," outlining the inner turmoil he feels about being called by God but rejected by his peers. Today's reading is a small slice of one of those passages. Jeremiah says he knows that even those closest to him want to get rid of him and have been hatching plots behind his back. That betrayal by family and friends is painful enough, but it soon becomes clear that Jeremiah is also battling against feeling that he has been abandoned by God, who put him in this position in the first place.

No prophet chooses the thankless and difficult task of speaking the truths of God in the face of obstinance and rejection. Only a true and deep sense of God's calling can sustain the prophet in these circumstances. And so, Jeremiah expresses confidence in God even as he struggles to feel as confident as he professes to be.

Isn't this true of many of us when we experience opposition or hardship as disciples? We would prefer to feel more sure-footed and courageous of heart. If we imitate Jeremiah and cry out to God with raw honesty, we may find ourselves once again on solid ground.

Meditation: Doubt is often portrayed as the opposite of faith, but in truth, apathy is much more dangerous. When in doubt of God's call, when frustrated by ineffectiveness or even betrayal in your ministry, care enough to speak honestly with God who will stand with you.

Prayer: God, you have called me by name. Strengthen me when I am weary, encourage me when I am fearful, and stand with me as I find my footing once again.

March 17: Fifth Sunday of Lent

Dying vs. Death

Readings: Jer 31:31-34; Heb 5:7-9; John 12:20-33

Scripture:
"[U]nless a grain of wheat falls to the ground and dies, it remains just a grain of wheat; but if it dies, it produces much fruit." (John 12:24)

Reflection: The Bible can sometimes confound us, but so can nature. When Jesus speaks about a grain of wheat, he draws from the natural world of agriculture, where germination and growth occur when seeds slip open and die. Dig up a plant such as wheat, and you will not find a seed; it is dead, but the fruit of that seed is healthy and living. Jesus uses this lesson from nature to teach his followers the meaning of his upcoming death.

Just as the death of a seed is not the final act in the seed's life, the dying of Jesus is not the final act in his life. It is a simple but profound lesson: life will come from death, and life will always have the final word. A simple lesson but not an easy one; dying is never easy. The dying of Jesus is not confined to the days of his arrest, passion, and crucifixion in Jerusalem. His dying begins as he is hounded and laughed at by detractors, and betrayed by some who are close to him.

By using the word "dying" rather than "death," we remind ourselves that the process of letting go is continual.

We work on developing a healthy ego, and at the same time make continual efforts to let go of the ego's power over us. We pursue the security of our homes and families, and at the same time acknowledge that safety can be fleeting. We use our gifts to earn a living and provide for our needs and wants, and at the same time pray for a spirit of detachment from these material goods. With each of these small "dyings," we draw closer to Jesus, whose dying introduces us to the power of truly living.

Meditation: As we surrender the idea that we can control all aspects of our life circumstances, we experience the great freedom to live in the moment, seeking God's will in *all* circumstances. In this way, we learn that dying has no ultimate power over us.

Prayer: God of life, take our sufferings and dyings into your divine heart and transform them into a path to fullness of life.

March 18: Monday of the Fifth Week of Lent

Courage Flows from Truth

Readings: Dan 13:1-9, 15-17, 19-30, 33-62 or 13:41c-62; John 8:1-11

Scripture:
Even though I walk in the dark valley
   I fear no evil; for you are at my side . . . (Ps 23:4)

Reflection: With the help of genetic testing and other investigative tools, over 3,000 people have been exonerated of crimes for which they have already served years in United States prisons. It is estimated that there could be more than 20,000 current prisoners who were falsely convicted (roughly five percent of the prison population). In ancient times, the number in any given area would probably have been significantly higher as legal proceedings often included no more than an accusation with little investigation, and sometimes led to immediate execution, depending on the crime.

The story of Susanna from the book of Daniel is one such instance where a wrongful conviction would have led to execution. Fending off two men who were trying to sexually manipulate her was hardly believable once those men turned the story around and accused her of being with a man other than her husband. In the dark valley of looming death, without hope for a rescue, Susanna found courage in the truth of her own experience.

The Gospel today tells the story of a woman caught in adultery who does *not* appear to be falsely accused. She is facing her local executioners, who seem willing to stone her to death, when Jesus disrupts their plans. In this instance, Jesus holds up a figurative mirror to the crowd, challenging them to self-examination, laying the truth of their own misdeeds before them. The woman finds courage to stand before Jesus in her sin and receive his forgiveness.

Meditation: Dark valleys come in all shapes and sizes, daring us to crumple to the ground in fear of what others may do to us or of what we do to ourselves in sin. Both women in today's readings are prepared to fall into darkness, but the truth sets them free, as it does for us as well. How will we respond to the truth of who we are and what we have done or failed to do?

Prayer: O God, give me the courage to stand up for truth, even should it cost me something dear. And when I discover the truth of my own failings, help me to trust that you will restore in me the courage to sin no more.

March 19: Saint Joseph, Spouse of the Blessed Virgin Mary

Daring to Hope

Readings: 2 Sam 7:4-5a, 12-14a, 16; Rom 4:13, 16-18, 22; Matt 1:16, 18-21, 24a or Luke 2:41-51a

Scripture:
[Abraham] believed, hoping against hope, that he would become *the father of many nations* . . . (Rom 4:18)

Reflection: It is an odd phrase: "to hope against hope." It would seem to mean that we do not hope at all, but it in fact means that we hope against all odds. We exhibit grit and determination even when something seems impossible. We step into the shoes of trust and keep walking in the direction of what has been promised.

The Bible tells the story of Abraham in just this way. He is advanced in years as is his wife, but God promises them numerous descendants and a land of their own. Abraham not only dares to hope but doubles down on the promise by pulling up stakes and setting out for an unknown place, acting solely on the word of the God he cannot see but whom he trusts all the same.

So many biblical stories reinforce this kind of raw hope in God. Such hope is rooted in a deep knowing and trusting that, as Julian of Norwich would say centuries later (and T. S. Eliot would echo), "All shall be well . . . because there is a force of love moving through the universe that holds us fast and will never let us go."

The hope that sustains us is strikingly visible in the life of St. Joseph, whose feast we celebrate today. He has legal options open to him upon learning that Mary is pregnant prior to their marriage: he could divorce her quietly or have her stoned. Instead, Joseph's own encounter with God allows him to hope against hope that all will be well. He chooses hope over vengeance, hope over shame, hope over improbability.

Meditation: The season of Lent is often portrayed as a long dirge, focusing on our sinful unworthiness. Maybe we should shed that image and instead see in Lent the opportunity to double down on hope, knowing that our sinfulness is no match for God's mercy, and our doubts are no match for God's firm resolve to save us.

Prayer: We hope in you, O God. Root us in the shocking realization that you choose to accompany us in every circumstance of our lives so that we are always firmly grounded in your love.

March 20: Wednesday of the Fifth Week of Lent

The Question of Authority

Readings: Dan 3:14-20, 91-92, 95; John 8:31-42

Scripture:
". . . I did not come on my own, but [God] sent me." (John 8:42)

Reflection: Have you noticed that the question of authority is a universal concern? A child puts his hands on his hips and proclaims to his babysitter, "You are not the boss of me." Teenagers push the boundaries of parental control, longing to have authority over their own lives. Politicians might question the need for checks and balances, or even the need for a constitution that protects freedoms by limiting certain powers. Those entering religious life often struggle with adapting to the norms and expectations of those who have authority in the community.

In today's Gospel account, Jesus is speaking not to those who oppose him but to his fellow Jews who believe in him. They question whether his teaching harmonizes with their understanding of their religious tradition. In particular, they wonder how Jesus can assume they are not free if they are children of Abraham. What follows is a defense of Jesus' authority. Jesus asserts that his very presence with them is due to God sending him. The authority of Jesus, and of his teaching, is derived from his Father.

Even as faithful followers of Christ, we sometimes fall into the trap of questioning his authority in our lives. So many cultural messages vie for our allegiance; it can be difficult to remember that the ultimate authority in our lives is the Good News of Jesus Christ. His word always frees us from whatever false standard is offered by the world in which we live. It takes a discerning heart to recognize the voice of Jesus and great courage to put his words into action.

Meditation: The word "authority" is derived from the Latin term for "originator," or the middle English word for "author." The one who has authority in our lives is the author of our lives. Who better to know how we will flourish than our Creator?

Prayer: Creator God, when we come to you with hands on hips questioning your authority over our hearts, remind us that it is you who fashioned our hearts, who created our minds, and who guides our moral lives. Give us the freedom that comes from listening to you.

March 21: Thursday of the Fifth Week of Lent

Reimagining Time

Readings: Gen 17:3-9; John 8:51-59

Scripture:
. . . "Amen, amen, I say to you, before Abraham came to be, I AM." (John 8:58)

Reflection: Our worldview is usually quite linear. Generally, things have a beginning and an end, events proceed in a sequence, and we picture time as a line going from one point to another. On the surface, this way of perceiving reality makes very good sense.

Some cultures around the world perceive things less as a series of events in a straight line and more as an enduring circle of relationships. From this point of view, all things are connected, regardless of time or location. Living a full life within a linear worldview is often associated with achieving goals and moving on to the next goal; within a relational worldview it's more about building and maintaining healthy relationships.

Jesus is often challenged by those around him who compare him to people like Abraham or the prophets. They assume he is claiming to be on a par with the great figures of faith who have gone before him, and they wonder where to fit him into the sequence. When Jesus answers them in today's reading from John's Gospel, he shocks them in at least two ways. First, he says that he existed before Abraham, certainly not a linear way of positioning himself. Second, by claiming to be "I AM," the divine name revealed to Moses, Jesus is claiming divinity. This claim takes him well beyond linear categories altogether!

While this terminology would not have been used at the time, Jesus is inviting those who come to him to step out of a linear worldview and instead see the world from the edge of eternity and through the lens of relationships. We too are invited to forge a healthy relationship with our ancestors in faith, not by making them into idols, but by seeing in them the work of God who is before and after all things.

Meditation: Lent is an ideal time to call to mind not only the public figures of faith who have gone before us, but those among our own families and friends who have been faithful examples to us. Their witness to Christ is ongoing, not limited to a particular time or place.

Prayer: Eternal God, may our lives be measured not by the accomplishments we mark over a lifetime, but by the relationships that are an enduring witness to your life in us.

March 22: Friday of the Fifth Week of Lent

Calling Down Vengeance

Readings: Jer 20:10-13; John 10:31-42

Scripture:
. . . Let me witness the vengeance you take on them,
  for to you I have entrusted my cause. (Jer 20:12)

Reflection: I will be honest. I am uncomfortable with Jeremiah calling down God's vengeance on his persecutors. I am ill at ease with such language and with the enterprise of watching one's enemies squirm while getting their just desserts. But I do not believe we can simply choose to ignore such passages in our sacred writings.

Many years ago, I set out to read and pray my way through the book of Psalms, thinking I would be edified and inspired by the prayer of God's people. And I was to some extent. But I soon discovered that the language of vengeance and complaint was laced all throughout the 150 prayers. I didn't want to pray that the children of my enemies would be smashed against rocks as in Psalm 137, or that God would smash in the teeth of the wicked as in Psalm 58. It seemed presumptuous of me and contrary to my own experience of God's mercy.

Over time, I have come to appreciate a few things about this language in our Bible. First, we often use hyperbole, or exaggeration, to make a point. We might feel sunk in a swamp of despair or feel that we are drowning when, in fact, there is no swamp or water nearby. Could the language of vengeance also be a bit of hyperbole? Second, I recognize that I pray from a different place than someone who is persecuted or neglected, or those whose town has been invaded by enemy forces. When I pray with these vengeful passages, I try to give voice to experiences that are not mine but that reflect my awareness of the larger community. Third, who am I to deny anyone the right to freely express to God what they honestly feel? Certainly God is big enough to take our anger or despair or pain, and wise enough to transform it.

Meditation: What situations in our current world might cause people to plead for God to take vengeance? Could your response to injustice become part of God's answer to such prayer?

Prayer: O God, may our hearts ache for your justice, the justice that defends the poor and strengthens those who are outmatched by their circumstances. May our firm resolve to right wrongs always bend to your will, and may our prayers be honest so you can work with the real situations of our lives.

March 23: Saturday of the Fifth Week of Lent

The Fullness of Time

Readings: Ezek 37:21-28; John 11:45-56

Scripture:
They looked for Jesus and said to one another as they were in the temple area, "What do you think? That he will not come to the feast?" (John 11:56)

Reflection: One spring I kept an eagle eye on the dogwood tree near our front walk. Every day I snapped a photo of the same branch filled with tight buds, then gradually opening, until finally the full blooms filled the branch. What I really wanted to capture was that moment when the early bloom turns from lime green to milky white. The dogwood itself "knew" when this was happening and put on quite a show when the time finally came.

I can't help but think of that image when pondering how often Jesus talks about his "hour" or his "time" in the Gospel of John. As this hour he speaks of draws near, Jesus draws near to the heart of Jerusalem, the temple. The divinity of Jesus will be revealed fully through his passion, death, and resurrection, and in John's Gospel, Jesus knows to wait until the time is ripe, just as the dogwood bloom waits until just the right moment to reveal its beauty.

Today's passage from John places Jesus in the capital city just before the feast of Passover, which is also the time when plots to kill him are reaching a fever pitch. We are told that he leaves for a time to stay in the desert, avoiding the public. Jesus knows his time is near but not quite yet, and he will not be rushed by fear, frenzy, or ego.

Meditation: The feeling of today's Gospel can be captured by the expression "when the time is ripe." Just as a farmer knows the signs to look for in advance of the harvest, so Jesus looks for the signs that God's people are ready to receive him, ready to see even in his suffering that God's saving love will bear the fruit of salvation.

Prayer: What wondrous love, Jesus, that you would give yourself as a redemptive sacrifice for us. Teach us your way of reading the signs of the times so that we too can be prepared to offer ourselves in service and sacrifice. Draw us into the depth of your love so that we are always ready to receive your revelation.

March 23: Saturday of the Fifth Week of Lent

March 24: Palm Sunday of the Passion of the Lord

Testing our Enthusiasm

Readings: Mark 11:1-10 or John 12:12-16; Isa 50:4-7; Phil 2:6-11; Mark 14:1–15:47 or 15:1-39

Scripture:
Peter said to [Jesus], "Even though all should have their faith shaken, mine will not be." (Mark 14:29)

Reflection: I am struck by how often Peter, one of Jesus' first disciples, expresses great enthusiasm for Jesus and his mission. When Jesus walks on water, Peter tries it too. When Jesus is transfigured on the mountain, Peter is ready to set up tents so they can stay there, basking in the light of revelation. When Jesus asks his closest followers if they will abandon him as others have, Peter replies, "Master, to whom shall we go?" (John 6:68). And now, on the eve of tragic events that will lead to the crucifixion of Jesus, Peter proclaims that his faith in Jesus is rock solid and that he will even die with Jesus if necessary.

But enthusiasm only goes so far; it is tested by practical concerns, hardship, and even fear. Enthusiasm can be the kick-starter for great endeavors and, as in the case of Peter, authentic faith, but it is no substitute for the depth of trust that is required to see things through to completion. In our Gospel today, Peter discovers this in a very painful way as the original zeal of his pledge to Jesus melts away while he warms himself near a fire at the moment Jesus is being beaten and condemned.

The events of Jesus' arrest and crucifixion would test anyone's enthusiasm. But these events also call forth the courage to pay the cost of discipleship. Like Peter, we are invited and challenged to move from enthusiasm to deeper trust, and then to commitment. Faith is easy when we first fall in love with Jesus or when all is going well. But when tested, faith can become the reliable foundation of a lifetime of committed love.

Meditation: The events of Palm Sunday are revisited on Good Friday, providing bookends for the final week of Lent. Consider in this time how your own faith has been or is being tested, and consider how your enthusiasm for Christ has grown more solid and reliable.

Prayer: Jesus, when I first answered your call in my life I could not have known where it would lead me. Take my moments of enthusiasm as a pledge of hope in you. When I grow weary or fearful or even lazy in my walk with you, remind me of your faithfulness to the very end.

March 24: Palm Sunday of the Passion of the Lord

March 25: Monday of Holy Week

Judgment and Credibility

Readings: Isa 42:1-7; John 12:1-11

Scripture:
. . . "Why was this oil not sold for three hundred days' wages and given to the poor?" (John 12:5)

Reflection: Today's scene from the Gospel of John holds several lessons, one of which is about criticism and credibility. I have found in my own life that it is usually easier to criticize others and condemn institutional policies and practices than it is to do the kind of self-examination that will change my own behaviors and attitudes. I think there is a bit of that going on in today's story of the woman who anoints Jesus and the reaction of one of his disciples.

When Mary of Bethany anoints the feet of Jesus with costly oil, her action prefigures the anointing that attends a burial, indicating that she seems to recognize the significance of Jesus in their midst. Judas, the group's treasurer of sorts, objects to the costly wastefulness, supposedly out of care for the poor. But Jesus knows otherwise, and the Gospel writer makes sure we also know that Judas's concern is only for the money he controls. No matter how pious he may sound, his motives are far from charitable or honest. Therefore, his assessment of the anointing is not credible.

The stingy response of Judas stands in stark contrast to Mary's extravagance. Mary's anointing of Jesus gives credible witness to his identity, and Jesus' response to Judas that we will always have the poor with us does not in any way diminish his own commitment to those on the fringes, a commitment he demonstrated throughout his ministry.

Offering an honest critique of situations that we believe are unjust or hurtful is an essential part of being Christian, but it is equally important that we are committed to being part of the solution.

Meditation: One of the great temptations of our time is to stand in judgment of others, to tear down but not build up. It has become acceptable in almost any public forum to flippantly dismiss the experiences of others or rudely condemn their views and actions. In the process, we fail to exhibit the generosity of Christ whom we profess to serve and imitate.

Prayer: Jesus, as I recall your journey to Jerusalem, I stand in awe of your authentic witness to truth and charity. As I make my journey here on earth, keep me focused on you. May my words be a credible expression of love for your people, and my attitudes flow from living in right relationship with you.

March 26: Tuesday of Holy Week

The Power of Darkness

Readings: Isa 49:1-6; John 13:21-33, 36-38

Scripture:
And it was night. (John 13:30)

Reflection: The parents in the neighborhood where I grew up were all in agreement that "nothing good happens at 2:00 in the morning." They wanted us safely home hours before then, of course. They hated the thought of any one of us getting into trouble while out with our friends or getting into a car accident. And while these things can happen at any time of day, there is something about getting such a call in the middle of darkness that is particularly unsettling.

In today's Gospel passage, Jesus acknowledges, perhaps laments, that he will be betrayed. When Judas sets out from the last meal shared by Jesus and the Twelve, John makes sure to note that this was not a time of light, but a time of darkness: "[I]t was night." Perhaps our parents were right: nothing good happens in the wee hours of darkness.

But what if we consider that darkness has more than one dimension? In the darkness of the night, most of us find restoration in sleep. From the darkness of a mother's womb, a child is born. From the darkness of the earth, a seed breaks open and begins to send up shoots of life.

Judas's betrayal of Jesus is a dark and sinister act; it stands in stark contrast to the Gospel's description of Jesus as light shining in the darkness. But could Judas's act of betrayal also be the necessary time of darkness that will produce the glory of something new? Something substantially life-giving? Something worthy of the light of day?

Meditation: Quite often we fall into the pattern of painting with one wide sweep of the brush. A thing, a person, or an idea is either all good or all bad. We're more comfortable with these definite distinctions, some of which may be valid, but most of which are more complex. Could part of maturing as Christians be a willingness to acknowledge the "both/and" reality of our lives? We are sinners *and* we are saints. We are needy *and* we are blessed. The darkness we encounter can be both fearsome and life-giving.

Prayer: Jesus, light of the world, help us to explore the many facets of what it means to be human. Walk with us in darkness and in light so that we can recognize you in both and be assured or your mercy.

March 27: Wednesday of Holy Week

No Time for Apathy

Readings: Isa 50:4-9a; Matt 26:14-25

Scripture:
> . . . I might know how to speak to the weary
> a word that will rouse them. (Isa 50:4)

Reflection: In the Christmas hymn, *O Holy Night*, we sing, "A thrill of hope, the weary world rejoices, for yonder breaks a new and glorious morn." Both the coming of Christ among us at his birth and the crucifixion of Jesus at the end of his earthly life are marked in music and in our Lectionary by mention of "the weary." Our world's weariness is seen in sin and sorrow, in sickness and war, in ill health and injustice. We are as weary of dealing with our own inner turmoil as we are of seeing how evil seems to endure in the world around us.

The good news is that while we are weary and our world is tired, God does not grow weary and never tires of giving us reason to hope. The prophet Isaiah knows that the words he speaks to those who are weary in exile are the result of God's grace working in him. He sees Israel's sinfulness and knows that God will not give sin the final say. So, the prophet stands among the people, ready to accept their fear and misunderstanding, if only he can rouse them to wakefulness, if only their wakefulness will turn their hearts to the grace of repentance.

The danger of weariness is that it sets us on a path to apathy. We give in to feeling inadequate or overwhelmed and fail to see where justice is growing or where hope is being planted. This Holy Week is a wake-up call inviting us to join in rousing the world to something better.

Meditation: The life, death, and resurrection of Jesus awaken the world to the possibility of a kingdom where good and beauty and justice triumph over sin and despair. The work of this kingdom is given to those who are awake to the love of God. We are stirred to act on behalf of the poor, alerted to injustices that we can address, made aware of our own demons—all because God dares us to stay awake.

Prayer: Wake us from our apathy, O God. Provide strength to the weary. We hope in your kingdom and are ready to put our hope into action.

March 28: Holy Thursday

Serving Up Humility at the Last Supper

Readings: Exod 12:1-8, 11-14; 1 Cor 11:23-26; John 13:1-15

Scripture:
"If I, therefore, the master and teacher, have washed your feet, you ought to wash one another's feet." (John 13:14)

Reflection: Every year I get a little tickled, and a bit disheartened, when I see parishioners move forward to have their feet washed at our celebration of Holy Thursday. I'm convinced those feet have never been cleaner or more trimmed and polished than in anticipation of having them "washed"! It seems to me that we're missing an opportunity to explore the full symbolism of what is taking place in our parishes, and the power of this ritual to call forth the uncommon virtue of humility.

Both sides of a bowl of water and a stack of towels paint a portrait of humility. Jesus bends in service to his closest followers; he bows to their dignity as he washes away the dust of traveling across packed dirt and chipped rock. This gesture of welcome tells us that Jesus knows his own dignity is in no way diminished by serving those he loves, even serving one who will betray him. Perhaps Jesus hopes not only to clean their feet but to scrub off any stubborn resistance and rinse away any lingering doubts among his disciples.

Peter epitomizes all of us who struggle with humility. He feels uncomfortable to be on the receiving end of a task usually reserved for nameless servants; he feels unworthy of such an intimate gesture from Jesus. Peter's objection to Jesus washing his feet comes from a place of pridefulness or a false sense of humility. He does not seem to grasp what St. Thomas Aquinas realized, that humility means seeing ourselves as God sees us. When we see ourselves in this way, we become receptive to the grace of being served and becoming servants.

Meditation: This year, as you participate in the Mass of the Lord's Supper on Holy Thursday, think about the people who are having their feet washed. Consider all the places their feet have taken them: into factories and operating rooms, onto building sites, tiptoeing into the room of a sleeping baby, onto the field of sport, or through rows of newly seeded crops. Our feet are one way we interact with our world, putting into action the transformation our hearts experience through grace.

Prayer: Wash me, Jesus, with the grace of humility that will begin to cleanse me of selfishness and pride. In accepting your life of service for me, may I become a servant like you.

March 29: Friday of the Passion of the Lord (Good Friday)

The Humanity of Jesus

Readings: Isa 52:13–53:12; Heb 4:14-16; 5:7-9; John 18:1–19:42

Scripture:
And [Pilate] said to them, "Behold, the man!" (John 19:5)

Reflection: Do you recall the prologue of the Gospel of John where we are given a cosmic family tree for Jesus? Even before the first inklings of the universe, God's Word has been present and active, and yet we are told that this Word became flesh and "made his dwelling among us" (1:14). God, in Jesus, dwells with us, pitches his tent among us, and is in every way human.

Much later in John's Gospel, in the midst of the passion of Jesus, Pilate unwittingly proclaims the significance of the incarnation. He identifies Jesus with three simple words: "Behold, the man!" Pilate's intent is to demean Jesus, to draw attention to the inability of Jesus to avoid suffering and death. The Roman procurator of the region wants to demonstrate that this fellow from Nazareth is no more than a mere human being. Little does Pilate know that in God's great plan, the very humanity of Jesus reveals more about God's identity and goodness than any golden crown and royal robes could ever capture.

In this moment, Jesus is pictured simply as a man bandied about in the heat of violence and misunderstanding. His passion gives testimony to God's desire to embrace us, to enter into our world, even when it involves suffering and leads to death, both of which Jesus carries for us as he carries the wood of the cross through the streets of Jerusalem.

Meditation: On this Good Friday, as you venerate the cross, place yourself in the scene at the Roman praetorium in Jerusalem. Imagine the tone of Pilate's pronouncement, the way he intends to demean Jesus. And then imagine the dignity of Jesus as he hears the crowd call for his crucifixion. How will you use your own humanity to draw others to the God who is willing to risk it all for us?

Prayer: Jesus, we enter into the mystery of your loving us unto death. Help us to walk as you did, sharing with others the human condition, knowing that even in our dying to self, we are joining our sacrifice to yours.

March 30: Holy Saturday and Easter Vigil

Places of Divine Encounter

Readings: Gen 1:1–2:2 or 1:1, 26-31a; Gen 22:1-18 or 22:1-2, 9a, 10-13, 15-18; Exod 14:15–15:1; Isa 54:5-14; Isa 55:1-11; Bar 3:9-15, 32–4:4; Ezek 36:16-17a, 18-28; Rom 6:3-11; Mark 16:1-7

Scripture:
[T]hey saw that the stone had been rolled back; . . . "[G]o and tell his disciples and Peter, 'He is going before you to Galilee; there you will see him, as he told you.'" (Mark 16:4, 7)

Reflection: There are places in our lives that hold special meaning: the park where a couple got engaged, a hometown baseball field where a child played ball, the route we walked to school as children. I recently experienced this deep sense of meaning when I returned to a parish where I was a member for thirty-five years.

I was back in town for a funeral, and I realized through the course of the day that I knew all but two people who had gathered. In my pew, I could close my eyes and recall a variety of special occasions in that sacred space, or open my eyes and appreciate the architecture and muted colors of the tapestry. It was heartwarming to have such an emotional reaction to a place, and I later realized it came in part from seeing it as a place where I started my adult life and experienced maturing in my walk with Jesus and his people.

I wonder if the apostles experienced something similar when, at least in Mark's telling of it, they returned to Galilee where they would meet the risen Lord. Galilee was the place where they were called, the place where they first began to follow Jesus and witness how he interacted with people and revealed God to them.

Was Jesus inviting the apostles to encounter him in a fresh way in the familiar place where they first met? Would being in that familiar environment help them ponder more deeply all they had experienced so far, and ready them to continue the mission of Jesus?

Meditation: Consider the role of "place" in your experience of encountering the Lord. Are there significant places where you recall God's action in your life in an almost visceral or instinctive way? While we can never recapture an exact experience from the past, how might God use a familiar place to open your heart to a new and life-giving experience of divine love?

Prayer: Jesus, risen from the tomb, help us appreciate the places where we have come to know and love you. Mark them in the memory of our hearts, and as we revisit them in mind or in person, may we be refreshed in our commitment to live as people of the resurrection.

March 31: Easter Sunday: The Resurrection of the Lord

Trusting in the Power of Life

Readings: Acts 10:34a, 37-43; Col 31:1-4 or 1 Cor 5:6b-8; John 20:1-9 or Mark 16:1-7

Scripture:
[H]e saw and believed. (John 20:8)

Reflection: Seeing is not always believing. A bright light in the night sky could be a star or an airliner. A compelling work of art could be from an artistic master, or it might be a fraud. An empty tomb could just as easily be evidence of grave robbery as evidence of something supernatural. Yes, believing is often preceded by seeing, but deep-down, faith-filled believing requires more than eyesight.

The followers of Jesus brought physical sight to the tomb. They saw the evidence of a stone rolled away and burial cloths rolled up and put aside. They may have initially assumed that the body of their friend was disrespected even in death. But they had been shaped by their experience of Jesus and knew that everything about him stirred their hearts and ignited their imaginations to hope in what seemed unlikely or even impossible. That empty tomb was not evidence of a crime; it was evidence of the power of God to bring life where death once dwelled.

Faith certainly can be rooted in physical realities that our senses can detect; our senses can attune us to wonder and awe. But faith takes us further. It gives us the courage to leap into trusting in God's surprises. It helps us move from wishful thinking to investing ourselves in what we know in our hearts to be true: that with God all things are indeed possible.

Easter makes a promise, the promise that we will experience in our own bodies the fullness of life. Every sincere act of forgiveness, each act of service, and all forms of true worship ready our hearts for the fullness of the kingdom of God.

Meditation: An inspiring preacher once asked a jammed arena of Christians: "Are you Gospel people? Do you believe in the Good News?" When the crowd roared "Yes!" he responded, "Then tell your face about it!" How do our lives speak of resurrection? Is it clear to others that we carry the Gospel within us?

Prayer: Jesus, risen from the dead, give us the grace . . .
    of using our senses to see you,
       of knowing that you make all things new and all things possible,
       of trusting that your love for us leads us to fullness of life.
       In our living and our dying, may your Good News be proclaimed. Amen.

References

February 15: Thursday after Ash Wednesday
Kathleen Dean Moore, *Holdfast: At Home in the Natural World* (Corvallis, OR: Oregon State University Press, 2013), Introduction.

February 26: Monday of the Second Week of Lent
Timothy Radcliffe, OP, *What Is the Point of Being a Christian?* (New York: Burnes & Oates, 2005), 124.

March 9: Saturday of the Third Week of Lent
Pope Francis, *The Name of God Is Mercy: A Conversation with Andrea Tornielli*, trans. Oonagh Stransky (New York: Random House, 2016), 8.

March 18: Monday of the Fifth Week of Lent
For more information about wrongful convictions, see https://innocenceproject.org/.

March 19: Saint Joseph, Spouse of the Blessed Virgin Mary
St. Julian of Norwich, *Revelations of Divine Love*, chapter 76. The phrase "All shall be well" was popularized by T. S. Eliot in his 1943 work, *Four Quartets*, in the poem "Little Gidding."

March 28: Holy Thursday
St. Thomas Aquinas, *Summa Theologiae*, Question 161 (available on numerous websites).